Burned House with Swimming Pool

Burned House with Swimming Pool

poems by

Lisa Lewis

Dream Horse Press
California

Dream Horse Press
www.dreamhorsepress.com
Editor: J.P. Dancing Bear

Dream Horse Press
Post Office Box 2080
Aptos, California 95001-2080
U.S.A.

Lewis, Lisa
        Burned House with Swimming Pool
            p.100

                    ISBN 978-0-9821155-9-6
                    1. Poetry

10 9 8 7 6 5 4 3 2 1

First Edition

Cover: "STEPS" by Gini Holmes

In memory of my teachers

Donald Justice

Larry Levis

Henri Coulette

Contents

Burned House with Swimming Pool

Reason, or the ratio of all we have already known, is not the same that it shall be when we know more.

William Blake
"There Is No Natural Religion"

American Dream

It's the fastest way to cause myself big trouble.
But sometimes I wake on a sunny morning,
Nothing to do, nowhere to go,
Stuck in small town America, the hard crust of citizens
I imagine too little like me for us to know one another
Except in bad juju, political warfare
I'm destined to lose because I always have,
And it seems that if I could climb into a new SUV
Rich with perfume of showroom upholstery
And drive to a mall cylindrical and glossy as a space station,
I could stuff my shopping bags full to the jingle of plastic
Digitized in phone lines, checking my credit rating
And finding it secure, and I'd be happy.
My anxiety would bob against the bottoms of clouds
Like balloons flown from the fists of toddlers,
And when I finally made up my mind to go home,
My scruffy place on the avenue would be disappeared,
The rent house straitjacketed in mildewed siding
Not even the cemetery of dust balls I left behind
But never my life at all. Instead I'd return
To the farm I visited once, in my adolescence,
Those years before my mother married my stepfather,
When she still strove to support her parents and me
And the five horses we somehow acquired one by one
Because we lived in Virginia and that's what's done there,
As it is in Oklahoma, though it's different here,
With cowboys; we drove there with a realtor because this farm
On a mountainside an hour's travel from my grandparents' house

Was for sale, an acreage and a farmhouse,
Hullocks and hillsides, dips a girl could hide herself in,
Acting as she wanted in the film of her mind's eye.
Two of my friends who rode horses too kept company,
And while my mother chatted with the realtor we scrambled
Over rocks out of eyeshot down a steep decline
And smoked marijuana till time leaped into still focus,
Our laughter propelled into its frame and arrested
As we were not to be, secreted in freedom
And youthful adventure that afternoon
When my mother's responsible imagination
Neglected to guess what I was up to,
And the sun fostered our dreams together
Despite our usual rage at one another's habits.
She was talking about painting the attic
For my bedroom, my teenage sanctuary,
And I was toking a small ceramic bong on a daffodil hillside
With my buddies, giggling, anticipating hamburgers
At Macdonald's and later riding our horses without falling off
Because we'd be straight by then, without trouble
Of any kind—and we were right,
Though my mother's ambitions had overtaken her means,
Which is why she eventually married my stepfather
And after their Virgin Islands honeymoon that for as long
As the piña coladas lasted convinced her he was loaded
Everything went to hell—another story,
Not the joyous one I'm telling now and which I recall
Whenever I need to, apparently quite often.

She window-shopped downtown department stores—
When I was small she tugged me by the arm—
So the day at the farm with its antique barn,
Dried chunks of cow pie tiling the sills
Of stalls, merely extended the same dreamy practice
She performed faithfully as a second career.
Today, haunted by terror of getting in over my head with loans
As I had to just to survive for twenty years,
I wonder how wrong she was, since I can't kick the fantasies,
Urge to shop, to spend, American woman
Raised to fulfill my place in the system
Without a chance to manage it the marital way
Because unserviceable in the eyes of man,
Still flying the magic carpet of the pipe dream's liberties,
Pleasures of enhanced senses, bird calls
Drawling slowly as a southwest Virginia accent,
A packet of ketchup in the parking lot at Macdonald's
The funniest stunt in comedic history when I stepped on it
And it squirted its bloody contents up the white pants leg
Of an unsuspecting man who looked old to us girls, about thirty,
So we fled, hands clapped across our mouths
To stifle the hilarity, the joy, joy, joy of fighting back
Without hurting anybody, making our mischievous mark,
Demanding through it to have our way, why not?—
Wasn't that our American dream? Wasn't it?
The name of the county where that farm plowed its rocky soil
Against rippling hillsides is right on the tip of my tongue,
And the taste of failure too, hunger salty as ketchup,

Or blood, where I've bitten off the tip of desire, paradoxically
For cash to pay, as a good American must,
For anything I want to buy, though it's what I've fought
My whole life too, in that back yard of the macrocosm
Where I'm tolerated to live, to little notice:
It's good, and safe, I can laugh at myself and everybody else.
It's good the clouds still spin and bob, loopy
As the hopes of a bunch of stoned girls in the early '70's.
I haven't made the trip to Virginia in decades anyway.
I can still believe without cliché of understanding
Adults learn to compare like women about to be married
Showing off the double-debt of diamond rings.
It's just that it should've worked, what she wanted,
My hapless mother and her simple urge, honest as a bloodhound,
Decent without selling, to earn enough to keep us afloat,
Alone on a small farm high enough on the mountain
To keep its feet out of flood: I don't know how to measure
If I'm closer than she rose to a sky light years away.

Envy This

I thought myself fine, *fine*, the sunshine t-shirt slant above
My hips' widening, and was young enough
To pretend I didn't know the general gaze is drawn
To a gold figure. I must be remembering my stepfather,
Who hated me but stared, eyebrows a cloaking
Hood, so his bride, my mother, shoved me to the back
Steps where I stayed dressed for once, smoking
Cigarettes, stalling till my boyfriend arrived
To transport me to more boys and bad actions.
Each weekend a gang of kids drove to Charlotte
In somebody's battered Oldsmobile—bashed doors,
Sizzled dome light—huffing joints, seeking adventure
At rock concerts, and if the acoustics disappointed,
Promise beckoned like an echo. We gained
Speed on the highway, bounding over tracks,
Weaving through the standing crowd, Fillmore seating,
A glance torn from the stage a triumph. Boys slouched
Like hats: I was too dumb to suspect. Drugs weren't hard
Enough. Penises sulked, wadded in pants like tissues.
Later, clumped in a motel room, tough guys huddled
In bathroom, door locked, pumping up veins. They named
Their brand of penetration. I took what I could get.
So what a laugh, to live on with that behind me,
When pride noticed nothing subtler than a wah-wah
Or chin bristling with beard of a twenty-year-old,
Baggie in pocket, a line about Wesson oil and Quaaludes.
Match it if you can. I knew what I was doing, building
My reputation, to look back on, throw into the hollow

Sneers of gutless wonders decades later
Like a balloon swallowed to smuggle junk.
No computers then, piety, terrorism, blue uniforms
Scanning searchlights down rows of knees.
That was the life. It didn't hurt but winding down
Does, watching over my shoulder so I don't check out
What's ahead, calling everyone else coward, nowhere to go
From bright morning to envious twilight but down.

I Don't Want You To Take Off My Clothes

How do I tell you just by thinking about you, wobbling down the street
        on significant tires? You could wind my watch.
           You could hand over a cardboard box
      for me to fill with neckties. I'm not the gift behind the bow
you wear at your adam's apple. I'm not sure I want you to unwrap
      my corners, starting with a rip the size of a bee-sting and finishing
           with foil flung to the clouds, shining their bottoms like bacon fat.
But I'm beginning to sense movement in the woods where the kids whisper
      someone's buried. I'm starting to wish I could speak like an earplug:
         intimacy in murmur, matte sheen on ululation.
If I could draw a towel across your cheeks to wipe away
          your glaring me in the eye: don't ask how it turned up
      on your face instead of the chubby grocery store manager's
         in the mosaic apron. Apparently you longed to watch us unite,
     lips and fingertips and the bristling realities of catfish in the pan,
his offering on a Friday night when we might've viewed
      a sentimental movie. You're no innocent despite quaint modes
         of transportation, carving scallops in pavement all the way
to the boathouse. I doubt anyone
     can rid me of embarrassing palmettos, untouched
boardroom glasses (I'm serious about paying too much for the varnish)—
      except, did I mention it already, you, unbalanced one, you,
         who steal the neap tide, you, packed in a leather case
like a bar of ideological soap, you, nebula, you, shirt button, you, birth
      of the world, you, abalone, you, letter bomb battery running low,
        sedgegrass promising abandonment.
Forgive me my desperation. You're the only father I've ever loved,
     and if you were a tall drink of vodka, I'd toss you
        over my shoulder for luck.

The minute you turn your rectangular skull—carved from zebra stone—
        you'll find out what I'm after.
                Flashing out of my lowly corner like a newly healed leper,
I pause no longer than to catch a whiff and haul you into the pavilion
       where now we stand in my dream, figuring as best we can, peach
             or peapod? What's in this exhalation, anyway? Our diagnostic?

The Well-Intentioned

A man graying at his clipped temples
Reaches into his blazer pocket to sleeve
A checkbook bound in calf.
He offers to causes when he can afford it,
A gift to return, a policy, balancing per annum.
His wife lingers poised as if to shimmer
In flight to the edge of the mantel.
An ornament free of the impulse towards glitter—
Though in her hands, that could work too,
Like Russian salmon encrusted in walnuts
Roasted on a gold foil plank.
This dignified couple, dutiful to community,
Long to be in love with the future, mold it
Into their sculpted image, profiles hewn
By the blade or inherited from adventurers
Of previous generations. In the painted alcove
Of the historical building where today's fund-
Raiser has warmed and fed the local elite,
There is no danger—no mercury rising
In the thermometer of dream—
Of harm to anyone's confidence,
Not a scuff on the toe of a wing-tip slipper
Or a pulled thread in a sofa pillow.
The accoutrements might be spare, "moderne,"
Or chandeliers might shine like wealth
Of wars. The blessedly deaf
Don't mean to be rude when they don
Faces like powdered gloves from a box.

You could ask them forever what they mean
When they mean and they'd promise
Only be good. There's nothing to fear
Until someone avows *No personal animosity*—
The tone of voice milky, yet credible.
Then compasses point to an unstable pole,
Pounding rivers to the end of the world.
If some occasions are poisoned by enemies,
Some thaw as little as an ice sculpture
Spreading angel's wings over linen.
You can almost hear the clack of spine bones
On streambed stones: agate against striped agate.

The Woman Who Sued Me

There was always something funny about her.
When she smiled you had to think of a German Shepherd:
The tough bubble gum of flesh waxing the teeth together.
She said she had no time for me. I had my faults.
I knew she thought I was a reluctant administrator.
She caught me at my desk staring out the window
Instead of typing out orders or demanding resources,
And she longed to be an administrator her own way.
She would stop people from talking out of turn.
She would stop them from laughing at silly jokes
By holding up her forearms and hands in a T.
She had friends who didn't want friends
So it was good for them all to have a friend who didn't want
Friends either. They were people with time to dream
About the friends they didn't want, and when they talked
They talked about the people they dreamed about.
I had no idea they were dreaming about me,
Telling one another their dreams the next morning,
Reaching for cellphones on bedside tables
And the unlined notebooks where they'd jotted details.
I'll admit I always thought there was something funny
About the lot of them. They asked to be photographed
Beside the First Families and the guardians ad litem.
They devised codes of honor including warnings
Against taping cartoons to office doors. They served
House guests shallow dishes of skimmed broth.
They were deathly afraid of birds.
They never mentioned they had millions in the bank

But everybody said it was true.
I never repeated it, though I'll admit to hearing it
And liking it. I'll admit I still like the world
For its facts and its objectivity,
The way you can whack a chunk of wood in two
With something sharp and it falls apart
Like an eggshell a scary reptilian baby bird just pecked itself free of.
I like the vulnerability of the world,
It won't lie and say automobiles don't hurt it,
Nuclear reactors don't hurt it, rich people don't hurt it:
It just gets hurt and eventually we all die.
I like that you can live like the world if you want to
And take shit from movers and shakers
And show it all over your face and body:
You can look very hurt because you are,
Like the place I've read about in the north Pacific
Where discarded plastic grocery bags float in an island
Bigger than all the plaintiffs put together:
Somehow they found their friends out there,
The smothering tangle of everything false bound as one.
You'll have a scar everyone can see
And liars can lie about if they want to,
Or if it's useful to them, and they want it to be so it will:
But the best fact in the hard, factual world
So many people don't want to tell the truth about
Is that nobody can make you be one of them.
Instead there's the silver maple sucking the water
From the earth's surface so no grass grows.

There's the gelding in the north pasture
Who'll kick you right between the eyes
Or wherever else is handy
If you walk too close to his butt when he's grazing.
There's the lament of the stars obliterated by cloud
The night you decide to stay up late and name the constellations,
And the elegy to the last time you had a chance
To rescue a tortoise from a busy highway.
Today I don't know where the woman who sued me
Is carving her narrow path through a mob of admirers,
Or enemies real or imagined, or molecules, or oak leaves.
I know she will keep on harming me if she can,
As long as she hopes to take somebody's money,
And it will show on me, and I won't be able to stop it,
And there will be a lesson in the sight of it
And its various reminders to people in the know:
Good for us all to see what happens in the world,
Or to it, when someone claims she knows something
She doesn't really know and all those with similar arguments
Move closer to her like mosquitoes hover
Near the odor of animal breath.

Hendrix Redux

Again tonight the kids next door are rattling the panes with the music of my
        youth.

Thirty years ago those guitar crescendos on a tape deck paced the blood through
        my veins, the drugs too,

Secret as sneaker soles on a driveway, dread of police and nights in jail without
        bond,

Which most of us knew the hard way, so now I know that despite kindred
        gestures—like failure to meet me,

Older neighbor, in the eye—and hair and bellbottom jeans, they're not getting
        the moves right

Over there, they're way too chaste. I don't know if I'm smug for the sake of long-
        ago superiority,

Headlong passions the music sound-tracked and the young next door chase
        into strings, not guessing what's missing.

Wouldn't they hate to think it's me? Who memorized "Voodoo Chile" straight-
        faced past parody, its hero-author puking in the grave,

His image on the poster collection high school kids from miles around admired
        in the bedroom shrine

Grudged into my parents' house? I want to say we were the real thing, except I
        don't believe it, except I can't believe

Anything else, and isn't the tragedy that it's true, we were, now we're not, and no
        one is? Real is dead of old age

And t-shirt slogans declaring fifty the new thirty miss the point: that was always
        too old too?

If I think hard I still feel stainless steel pricking the skin over my vein, the clean
        race of chemical burn

Through my lungs, *goddamn*, the courage of making love to a needle and a
        skinny long-haired boy later in the hard-moon night!

Goddamn! Goddamn right! I might've shouted. I might still shout, though tonight
    I want to punish somebody
Young for not surpassing me like I believed then had to happen, proving me
    wrong like I never anticipated,
Proving by going nowhere that I went nowhere and linger there, grinding my
    molars,
Amphetamine to the stars; and Jimi's licks and chops and feedback, even then I
    was mourning for his long-necked hands
That never would caress anyone, especially me, honorably sorry I had just
    missed a groupie's love for that touch.
It was something you could think without shame, not these kids thirty-five
    years after his death
Playing at being him, don't they know to hang their heads? They do hang them.
    Even without the drugs, they hang their heads.
All day tomorrow they will shamble ashamed through the dusty November
    leaves,
Casting my glare from their tenderness, wondering what they missed or not
    wondering at all,
Since that may just be my business, same as when change yawned limitless
    and I wondered
How far we'd ride, me and my buddies, most of whose names I've forgotten by
    now—
I hope you don't believe that lie. It's going to be bright as a fresh scar tomorrow
    morning, and where will those kids be?
The kids I wish I could be honestly happy for, stupid as that seems, considering
    they probably wish I'd die.
I'm their worst enemy tonight, fuming about calling the cops and holding back
    because I spent some nights in jail

For doing what a freak girl had to do in 1972, and now I'm so glad for it I wish I
       could give it away to see it alive.

Bottle this shit, man, and sell it, it's far out. Like me, so long and drumming into the
       future

With those kids I can't love no matter how I try. And the loss they pound down
       my throat

In the otherwise still night, stolen but not used up, like hauling off somebody's
       fast, smooth car and not even trying to drive.

My Horses and I

My horses and I are staked out on the secret plains of Oklahoma.
Daily they wait for me to drive to them, bypassing
Blacktop, ash-heaps of logs simmering in late November steam,
Workmen striking matches in mist to make haste of waste,
Fire spinning wood to wind: I speed when the way is clear.

I sing to the ditches, Lay down my path through the darkness you guide
To its grave, patches of blackberry bramble, summer's infamy
Withered to weed-rows, gutted bodies of skunks, tortoises
Humbled by pickup tire: hidden, that's us, the horses and me,
Thick in winter fur blown brushy by winter wings.

A dozen Canadian geese on pond flash up when something rumbles—
Not fear. Maybe patience hammered into iron machine—
What anyone in her right mind needs to survive past solstice.
How long have we waited for this day, wet for safe burning,
Dry to spare flint and spark? The horses don't care,

Dreaming, as always, of the mouth's ritual pleasures. Chew,
Swallow, chew: lay me down. I'm prepared to stretch out,
Mark this spot, flanked by scatter of sawdust and dried apple.
I'm crouched on my heels, and the mare Jeanie searches my hair
With her muzzle, broad as a loaf. She wonders, and yesterday galloped

To my secret counting, *one two three one two three one two three,*
One denoting the beat of the gait in which the hind foot falls,
Striking off: no one notices but me, on our hillside where a wild turkey
Browses its natural sustenance and barn cats track gophers
In punishment for guttering the red earth, telltale wounds,

Promises I can't translate except as danger to gallop, counted or not.
When Jeanie's neck rose of her own will, I felt her jaw in the rein,
The snaffle clinked a chiming, and the joy that traced my fingers
Refused the name: the mare has agreed to offer because I ask.
When we trot across weeds, black grasses, seedpods, stems,

Tassels, blades like paper crackle to the touch, the word.
You might not believe when I swear it wasn't always this barren
Where I learned the wail of wind that might mean wait and see, or breathe.
My horses keep us alive as best they can. Jeanie neighs from her stall
And Abby picks her way through mud to the afternoon feeding:

She nudges me hard, paces a circle, peers at shadow because in the north
Pasture another mare whinnies. Maybe a striped hawk perches
Beside a fencepost. Maybe a horned owl or heron, both speak in tongues.
My horses and I are changed, here in the secret land.
Who looks but who must? Those born or otherwise forced?

The world is in retreat from courage, I say to the horses, inhaling clean air
Rushed in from mountains and sea to clash, tangling like twine
Around our ankles: it runs from the time we endure so well it's love.
It flees our hunger and our passions, difficult to fulfill. The horses
Concur as they spread the hay I throw them, and the sky is gray,

The wind is the sea, and nobody comes here, nobody bothers
What we do, stitched into resignation I compare to the sense in the belly
When errand or emergency calls you from the table,
But you know you'll return, to a spread of potatoes, ham, cheese, lettuce,
A knife and fork, and trouble within your capacity to repair.

Burned House with Swimming Pool

Likely turn up glamour here as richer treasures—
What you really wished for, food or clothing,
Not a swimming pool, its chemical green mix—
Algae, ancient city water, rubber liner, autumn leaves—
Poisonously hidden if you dare not peer between
Cracked slats once called "privacy fence," now
Simply symbol of past glory masking abandoned lot.
What if someone died here? Fire gnawed the far end,
Sparking, maybe, in tv antenna, hopelessly old-
Fashioned, dating this tragedy no one cleaned up or
Bothered to restore, a once respectable suburban
Dwelling flawed by relative grandeur where the neighbors
Owned no luxuries, so now it seems it burned to humble
Pride, a sin whenever it bursts past more modest,
Workmanlike comparisons. Our lives are worth
Nothing, after all, if they're not worth the same.
Here, in Oklahoma, though, they seem the same so
Seamlessly they're still just ciphers, swimming pools
Dangerous graves for next year's provenance, wasted
In a place like this, where nothing's safe but all is
Sacred. Or, at least, you'd think from reading bumper
Stickers, counting spires and storefront churches,
Overhearing mumbled prayers and testing higher
Literacy. The night this house burned down, who folded
Hands and begged God for mercy? Wife and mother?
Patriarch? Or children? Even the family dog's cracked
Dishes gather rain here still, as if that shepherd
Herded heaven's lambs now. This is what you get when

Fancy digs shame neighborhood demure. Here's hoping
Someone filed a settlement claim and spent the money
Leaving here forever, freed, euphoric: see, I would say
Otherwise, the opposite, suspecting arson, but I'd think it
Pat and moralistic, proof I too just need a fast way out,
Even charred and ruined, forsaking ownership for
Low roads. Not yet. Give me time, and I'll sear the good
Life without looking back, like backyard steak in summer,
Squealing kids in pool, a round of bridge planned at eleven.

Oklahoma

I moved here for a job. I rented a house on a busy street.
Around the corner, bars and a bagel shop. Young people
Walked the streets all night. They smashed beer bottles
And practiced guitar in garages so the roofs caved.
I taught myself to sleep with the tv on to drown out the noise
With the noise of the homogenous nation, not the town,
The kids from the country, sure they'd hit it big
To make it to the university, the ag school, second string.

Every time I went to the video store all the copies of *Oklahoma!*
Were rented. The students won prizes for scholarship
On *The Grapes of Wrath*. I'd never read it or seen the movie.
When I talked to strangers on the phone in the East
They asked if I lived in a tipi. When I drove to the City
I passed through reservations but saw only cedars
And open pastures, rolling out flat, abandoned, unloved.
I could smell disappointment steaming from thistle, leadplant,
Cottonwood, hollyhock. Who died? Coyotes hanging
From fences, murdered by a shot to the head. Turtles rushing
Across highways so pickup trucks crushed them on purpose.
Armadillos, suicidal, leaping up to meet their demise
Like born-againers whose women are barred
From attending college. And the women, the Indians,
Halfbreeds passing for white, generations passing,
Dying with their secrets, easy to do in shingled shacks
On rutted red clay roads behind the wind, and the dust
Now believed a curse of the past that could not
Kill again, everybody knows better

About planting, and plowing, and the used up soil, it's better
With bone ground in it, blood dried in it,
Brains gone mean, like Henry Fonda in *The Grapes of Wrath*
I finally watched the other night. He's not mean
From being in prison. He swears to his Mama
That didn't happen to him, then he proves it true.
The Joads were driven from Sallisaw, near Webbers Falls
Where a month ago a bridge over I-40 collapsed
Into the river, hit by a tugboat. Tom Joad's Grandpa,
The night before he dies, sobs on the step of the house to be razed
Next day at dawn, *This dirt ain't no good, but it's mine.*
He lifts a handful to sift through his curled fingers.
It's so grotesque it's funny. I could've said it myself.
Maybe it's what cowards say in Oklahoma, and if someone tries
To force them out they refuse by dying.
They have a mission, to pack the bad dirt rich
With their bodies, but their bodies are poor,
Breath blown away on the wind. Here when the living
Try to help the living they drag them down.
When they die they're not even nourishment for worms.

I might wake up and this safe neighborhood
The local realtors call College Gardens could be drifted in dust,
Traced with those wavy snakelines the wind draws
On the beach and in the red dirt where no rain falls
Except in deluge to wash away everything
And not soak in on its course south to humid Texas.
The movie's a window into the far away, like the Kansas State

Website where I watched film of dust storms in the thirties,
A man leading a mule by a wire fence, his hand reaching
And seizing fast, never letting go or they'd be lost
Like the houses with dust piled to the windows, tractors
Buried like shipwrecks' bones. You'd have to be crazy
To believe that could come back tomorrow.
But the first time I heard someone say, when the sky darkened,
"That front's in Kansas," I laughed. Who would try to kid me
Like that, we're hours from Kansas, you can't see that far!
Now when it storms I turn on the tv, that other little window
I press my face to, trying to see what's coming, and there's
Ponca City, an hour's drive away, and the lightning's bright
In the back yard, thunder's drowning the insipid music
On the Weather Channel: when the storm's there,
It's here. But unless it tugs over us like a blanket it doesn't rain.

In California they hated the Okies so much they called everybody
Who was poor an Okie. In Oklahoma they hate the Okies so much
They can't make the red dirt better, and in town
The good people who hate Okies shop at one grocery store
And the bad people who are Okies shop at another.
I shop at the one where the Okies go. The hood of my car's
A red dirt plain. I wash it when I have to go somewhere
People don't wear scarves over their mouths to step outside,
Or lose their voices at night because they worked
In the grainy sun, even if it's the ragweed
And not the dust, even if it's the sky that opens
Everything up close no matter how far it is.

I don't expect anybody to feel sorry for me,
Which should tell you how long I've been here.
Even the way I sing to birds has changed. The sky wheels
With striped hawks and redtailed hawks and scissortails
And mockingbirds and red finches and flocks of robins
Too wild to hop in front yards listening for worms.
I sing to them and they sing back. They recognize me.
They see like I watch a movie on the Internet,
From afar, knowing it's as real as it's going to get,
And it could be closer than it seems, they'd better live it up,
And if that means singing back to the woman driving
To the tallgrass prairie preserve and parking her little car
Far from all the pickup trucks and nearly falling to her knees
Before all that melancholy, that flatiron sky
That presses down and lets you see things you ought never see,
Secrets you ought not be in on, without ever getting close
So you always feel lonely too, well, they'll do that.
It's about all that's left besides flying and building nests
In the grass. I can't do those things. So I'm singing
A lot these days, and you're overhearing me,
And if it sounds joyous to you, it's because I've been driven crazy
By the wind, and if it's sad, it's because every word is true.

Swanky

Last night, late, a biography of Sharon Tate on A&E,
Stills of the sleazy little horror flicks she starred in
Framing her much-discussed cheekbones, a clip of Roman Polanski
Addressing an audience, his voice catching
On the words *Everyone knew how beautiful she was,*
But not many knew how good—I felt it rise like a perfumed cloud,
The muted geometry of 60's swank, martini glasses,
Tuxedos, swaths of black eyeliner, carpeted stairs
Into sunken living rooms, and a massive mahogany console stereo.
If you were a sexy doll you'd pad in stocking feet to tilt its lid,
Lilting a sideways glance to the purr of guitars and clarinet,
The voice of Dean Martin or Sinatra, this, *sophistication,*
Manhattan, London, longing, *moderne.* You could peer
Through a keyhole to the city skyline, cut away to the room
With that sleek furniture, a Persian cat leaping to the arch
Of an armless chair: to say I want it would be untrue.
It's not something I or anyone could want, not now,
Except as designs in catalogs styled *retro* or *vintage.*
But once I believed in it as basis, aspiration,
Believed with a child's naïveté in its permanence,
Believed my mother, who had passed through its door
Like a thread through the needle's slit, and could return
Any moment she gave up living too busy, as she always lived
Too busy for me; believed in it even as an adolescent,
When already it smacked passé; believed it bitterly, as with bitters,
As in the orange-slice old-fashioneds my stepfather plied me with
For his own reasons so I practiced padding barefoot
On carpet to slip into the half-bath in his *bachelor pad*

The months he courted my mother, and emptied them
Into the sink; believed it of him, who weighed so much
The year he dieted to save his life and charted his progress
On a sheet of lined paper taped by the scale he penciled
60, 59, 58, 56, day by imperceptibly leaner day,
So *no one*—meaning my mother, meaning me—could read
That ponderous, premier digit, the first time
I spoke the word *Coward* of him and was punished
By my mother's silence like a seal; believed it because his money
Bought a key to the *Playboy Club*; because he'd been photographed
With *bunnies*, their stiff satin suits high on the thigh above fishnets,
Their smiles varnished, eyes blank beneath the swank signature,
Spider lashes: believed it when I fought it, my contempt directed
Like a warhead against it, imagined I would defeat it, I a soldier
Versus doom, had no notion it had to die as every fashion
Passes in time to be replaced by some reconfigured cache of designs
To stimulate supply and demand, so each generation
May purchase its vision of its own dream, whatever
It's coaxed to desire: I believed. I did not associate the look
With the times but with truth. And as the 60s died
With Sharon Tate, and the rumor circulated I had no reason to doubt
Until last night the voiceover declared it false—that her nine-months
Fetus was slashed from her belly by the Manson clan murderers—
It lived on in me, like a hymn, or the earth and sky,
Same every springtime, dappled blue, forever familiar
When echoed by emblem, perhaps an *elbow-length glove*,
Worn with a *strapless gown*, cut above the knee, to swivel
With the hips, ah, so *classy*, whatever I thought that meant—

It's still in there, that memory, music, matte sheen, now
With the overlay of knowledge, which saddens, moving me along
The conveyor of years, scrambling to keep my balance, considering
Where I'm heading and why I believed; and nothing, no matter
How satisfying, stately, syncopated, objectively rare, kind, and right,
Like water or the finish of silk in my palm or all I've lost
Never to regain will challenge its station, naïve belief,
Sense of reward: I would grow to it, it would fall
Into my hands, and in some empty pocket of me
I'll always wait for that triumph, long after
Everything alive in me has withered inside its physical shell.
I will go with a scarf in sarong at my hips, pointing my toes
In stocking feet, posing before the console, dimming the lights
With a twist of the wall switch, thumbing through the platters,
Dusky Spanish guitars, snares: *put that record on.*

Autumn Uncovers the Tall of the Trees

I have not experienced that particular yearning.

Behind me the sister oaks shed drifts of November amber.
I imagine they're fast, uninterested in burdens,
including children.

The mothers shut me out. They want me to think
they spirit something beyond knowledge.
They speak of their hearts like green glass
polished to reflect me back into my own eyes
cast iron—chilly and quick to rust.

Then what? No one to remember me?

However, I fancy myself a curiosity in my own right.
From the ground up to my empty hands,
I'm odd as a vase soaked in water.
Keep going. You require the answer to me: of me.
You've tried to pretend otherwise.

Just look at me, on my sofa cushion, quite the spectacle,
not a mistake to my name.

I have what I need.
Nothing tires me but the ring of chimes
up the hill, always high-pitched,
so it's hard to hear the sisters letting their little leaves go.

Dear Late Snowy Morning

Forgive me for writing instead of showing up.
Our meetings in the garden remain my chief pleasure—
Baring my head to the high heavens and kneeling to touch
Earth, curling fern, granite and daffodil,
Apricot pit spat from trash can, fender of starling-
Spattered car, roaming tailless cat—whatever.

Today one look out the window staved off habit.
I woke to crackling on the sill—fine ice, its slick lit dull
Under cloud. Last night's local television listed church
Closings for good reason, not that sanctuary
Of pew and altar occupies me in clear weather.
Today's fresh because I'm same as the neighbors—

Home all Sunday, for once, and if they muse
On God, I match them: hard not to nowadays, no matter
If it's faith or fitting in that fishes prayer book
From high shelf and puffs the dust off. At night I channel-surf
And there's Joel Osteen preaching in a stadium,
His long jaw horn of plenty praise: *You're wonderful*,

He says, wide-armed, and seems to mean it. *Jesus thinks
You're wonderful*, which makes sense if you need it to:
The camera scans the crowd's faces, serious
With awe of self, the curtained stage, thousands of seats
Slicing down to the slim antithesis of Jonathan Edwards
Offering God's love for nothing. He leans at the podium,

Spotlight sunbather: in another life he'd flick cigarette
Ash to the floor for someone like me to sweep.
His wife seethes through smiling teeth to shill sermon cds.
I'd let the happy couple go as harmless business:
Caveat emptor. But their customers stuff pamphlets
Sealed like subpoenas in the hinge of my front door,

Omnipresent as the old idea, God's everywhere among us,
Defining me this minute praying to late snowy morning,
Spinning the world to fundamental simile:
Breath of breeze and sky's cathedral and F5 twister
"God's finger." If you were lonely you might feel wanted
In the company of man's image: never mind privacy,

The tender madness of speaking aloud to no one
Or wincing at your own footsteps crisp in the frozen grass,
Singular whisper on winter's face, like skates on a pond spray
To a stop, but life goes on. I don't require importance,
Large or small, godly, angelic, or devilish: a relief,
Since none's forthcoming for her who trips over steeple's

Shadow in the rush to make it home alone, and swears
Hellfire. Damnation. I've had enough. Get real—
Talking to no one, seraphim of air, the very twigs that last week
Almost burst burgeoning spring a month too early,
Thanks to unseasonable heat I consider human fault,
Along with the rest, better and worse, ideas, emblems, caricatures,

Organs, promises, curses, courts, and congregations
Flocking to claim otherwise in such mass that everything
Else we might divine together is cast out or nailed up.
The next thing we know, it's afternoon. Late snowy
Morning's gone and melt's warming, minus time for choiring
The coming months like locusts that swarm the land

And leave behind stripped and empty fields.

Come-Back Spell

I've never said this to a friend before: it's best you go.
It's best you stay away. I imagine you stepping
Over the threshold of a birdhouse. You're down to size,
You fit, you squeak by. Inside's a basket woven
Of twigs for you to cast out, you'll knit your own bed.
That's one way to get rid of you. Another is a dream
In which I'm playing bingo. My card's nearly empty,
I'm straining to hear the caller, and you stroll in,
That jet lag look on your face you wore
Before the future's promise rose like a glass wall
And you scaled it in iron shoes. You say
I must've taken a wrong turn and I say *Now I can*
Start winning, scrambling to my feet so hard
My chair's cloven hooves scruff a trough in the linoleum.
If I'm going to dream you out of place, I'll paint
Myself a plane to treat you to a business jaunt:
You'll tumble from the slotted belly onto fields
Plowed in cursive, a legible signature. I'll dream you
Checking your confident agenda, trajectory
Of opportunities. You'd have to be stretched
And snapped straight to fit the round door
Of the birdhouse, like thread a wren snatches
From the shoulders of your coat the last chilly morning
Of spring. You'd better hurry, I heard voices
Down the street. I'll unlatch the window and you'll slip
On the sill, claws flaking the frame, or maybe you'll leap
Knees tucked like a stag: my task will be to talk about it
Where you can't hear. I'll shovel holes in the ground

To fill with all the dirty words you mispronounce.
You know how I am: every syllable stitches me
Into your heart, needle notching the valve, so you can't
Breathe into your own balloon: you don't even want to.

We Couldn't Be True

Nothing would do him but to build that big house.
When it was still talk and plans on paper,
Maybe he couldn't tell. Maybe it shocked him too
When the freshly dug basement gaped in the hillside,
The workmen smirking as they lounged
Long breaks. Who could blame them?
Too much work for the pay, and what could it buy?—
Not enough compared to that hole, wide and deep
To bury us all if we lay down dying from embarrassment.
Maybe it was in the finished living room he told my mother
He thought I was faking my ridiculous accent,
Or maybe at the wet bar, the faucet's swan neck
Spitting into collins glasses, or in his study
With its plaid carpet and bookshelves empty
Except for his grandfather's medical library,
A West Virginia country doctor's. No use
Begrudging any of it, but I did, seventeen and too shy
To speak to adults because they looked at me funny.
I wondered how to act tough enough no one would notice
I flinched when they smiled because I wasn't like them
And couldn't change: all I wanted in life
Then, to erase the difference, even to know why
It mattered, since it seemed each grown-up varied,
Wizened grandmothers, fat grandmothers,
Prissy church-going grandmothers, mothers
In lime-green corduroy slacks driving station wagons,
Mothers with hair pinned pouffy in buns, tight
Skirts stringing their knees together, skinny redneck

Fathers who by age forty had sprouted breasts
Pressing against their tank tops ashen with sweat,
Big-bellied white-collar fathers chewing cigars
And never giving a thing away, and children
My age or younger: if you knew anything
You could already see what we'd be
In a year or twenty. My mother and I huddled
In my bedroom in the far wing of the big new house
And wept together in secret, though it didn't stay
Secret once she had to cook dinner and he saw
Her face and she sniffled I'd been *uncouth*.
I'd tiptoe to the pantry corner and hear him tell her
How to handle me, and later she'd try to practice
His advice. But because I was prepped I could withstand.
I'd devised my plan, nothing they could take from me
Would make me change. If they said I couldn't go out
I'd slip through the window, and if I scraped my thigh
Bloody on the rotating crank it would heal soon
Enough for my paranoid padding down asphalt
Hot from the summer day to my best friend's house,
Her room in the basement with its own entrance.
All our parents had set us at a distance.
We suspected the worst but who'd believe us?
What crime did our parents commit, not loving
Their ugly adolescents I know I'd fear if I had them today?
It was no lie for my mother to tell me he thought
I faked it, but the long sentences, inflated rhetoric
Of teenage melodrama, dried inside me like worm

Castings, whatever came out of me I'd imagined
True as stone declared fraudulent, my southern accent
I'd hated since hearing my voice on tape
In third grade, loud and flat, not a child's, not a girl's,
Not musical piping, tinkling of tiny bells,
But hammer on anvil. My mother used to threaten
To call Libby, a relative on her father's side,
Because I had to be a throwback: genetically the voice
Of Libby had possessed my throat, and I should talk
On the phone to Libby so I'd know how
I sounded to the world. I don't remember her
Making the call. If she did I couldn't hear
Myself in Libby so handed the receiver away
And ran to my friends who didn't remind me
How odd I was. Either they were too dumb to notice
Or even odder themselves. It's better not to remember
What you wanted to escape and finally did,
But it's also good to think what you couldn't guess
At the time, like why a man from North Carolina
Would have something against a southern accent
Or not be able to admit his own, which I couldn't hear
Then because I'd never heard anything else,
But now I remember how it sounded, not like mine
But also stupidly southern, and I understand why
He had something against me and worked against me
Every way he could. By now I've heard from other
People of similar lives, war among relatives
By marriage, which means newness and breaking

Habits, not the trouble of deeper reasons. Maybe
There are no deeper reasons. Which would make
Everything fake, a show that can run a long time
And never stop drawing a crowd, or what about
Those shifts people like to believe impossible, someone turning
Different overnight, they traveled to a new place,
Leaving everyone who knew what they were
So they could be anything they wanted? Now sometimes
People who want to flatter me tell me I seem *very real*,
Not like the ones who are so goddamned pretentious.
They mean they're glad I have a southern accent
And they believe what's said of southerners:
We're a little slow, relaxed, perverse, with a sense of humor
If you don't step onto our porches at night.
It would be good for other people if that were true about me.
I'll be damned if I know if it's true or not. You might
Doubt every last word about truth if you walked up
Somewhere you weren't expected and heard it all
Taken back or twisted some way you'd thought
Impossible, if what you were told before was true.
After all, a fact doesn't change in different company,
Because now the listener is fat, or old, or now the listener is
A rebellious teenager, and if anyone tells her rebellion
Is boring, another way of staying the same, she'll get mad
And you'll lose that much more credibility, the chance
Of setting her straight—whatever that means.
It means I didn't know a damned thing.
I still have the southern accent, but who'd believe it

Today if I said, *You know, I really don't know a damned thing.*
They'd think I must've learned something
Through all the trouble I talk about till I run everybody off,
Rolling their eyes like calves snubbed to a tree.
They might even get mad because I shouldn't be lying
At my age. But if I said, *You know, I sure do know a lot,*
Nobody would believe that either and they'd get mad
Because I shouldn't be so arrogant. So I'm back
Where I started, everything shutting down.
It might've been alive once, but now it's shit in the sun,
White scrim on top and dust underneath, and what he said
About my accent when I was seventeen and obsessed
With being good enough in the eyes of those unlike me
To make them stop noticing my feet or my hands
Or my nose or my teeth or my voice or my southern
Accent was just an idea, not his best but not his worst,
Since he lost the big house in a bankruptcy suit,
And we packed up everything the bank hadn't claimed
And lived on his oldest son's charity a while,
Something else for me to fight because I was sick
Of being ashamed. There was already so much
It could've filled that house's empty rooms
My grandparents died in and paid the overdue bills,
The workmen's shabby paychecks still too rich
For my stepfather to afford: it's all so long ago now.
Seemingly so fake. But that's just the trick
Memory plays when you've changed a lot
And you look back and think, *Was that me? Was it*
Really me? What the hell did I think I was doing?

Topography

The sky's white drawl slows the whole morning.
A crow calls from a clot of leaves, but its cry drops
Dumb as an eraser, and only one sparrow darts out
Of the grove, striking a path downward to clover
Curling the hill's cowlick. Little to spare:
Through indulgence and recompense, you hope
To defy the undeniable, what can't be known,
The eye's tunnel to the shape it's drawn to,
Where the surprise is only that every furling
Opens to look like you. Crow and sparrow,
Grass and hill. All measure lacking is distance,
Or raindrops tapping maple leaves, fingers
On piano keys, the iteration of farms seeping
Through town, boundaries perjured. Nothing
To pair you with: you're nursing a hold
On pineland, pinfeather, an arch of walnut
Branch hugging a slice of horizon. You're counting
Shapes that march up a gangplank to travel
Elsewhere, you can only guess: at least the ravine
Where the habit of seeds is taking root. So this
Is how it feels to float above the world: circles
And circles. Speed is of the surface. Belief
Borrows the shuffle of tires, and the ache of thorax
And sacroiliac knocks together as the right ache:
Bones in a sack. Knotted at the top. Thin twine,
Crochet unstitched and white as the sky's forgiving
Eye. It considers. Wide open, it spots you flying.

Little Despot

I knew him before I learned to pace the creaking floors
So the nailheads popped into my loafer soles.
He bowed like a nymph. I scooped him up in my palm
For a closer look. A bluish halo encircled his skull.
I hesitated to interpret its shape as evidence of the holy.
The more I stared him down—his curlicue eyebrows jutting
In the fashion of those with faith in their own mannerisms—
The rainier the day clapped my windowpanes flat.
We had come to an impasse of the arabesque.
Dispotto! I took care to grasp neither the limbs nor the grubby
Impudence, the squeaks of his knees grinding
The pudge of my thumb. I believed at that libratory moment
In the swaying of everything but the lid on his medicine bottle.
What's nuttiest about this story was my trust, the notion
I could put a stop to the future and his role as pejorist,
Which, if only I'd ascertained half I held beloved,
I'd've foreseen he'd cast on me, quitting his former station
And scribing between lines ever after the sparking
Of my demise, there, there, unjust as it was silver.

How to undo the calamity of the decades, uniforms
Folded in a bottom drawer, visits to shrines and popular
Graffiti? He's wending towards me as I waltz away,
A well-matched pair now I'm so often sloppier.
Alighting in distant fields, rising again on migratory swaths,
He's larger and swims the currents above, thanks
To brighter spheres bursting in the interim.
Once I snapped a garter around my thigh, strode away

On the pang of all I thought to be spoonfuls of doses,
Minds. It seemed little enough to expect from the marsh,
The demure feathers of loons. Now he swallows me,
Sudden as a globe spinning at the forefront of a congress.
I'm an apricot in the master's mouth. That's his palate,
Warm and impassable, a trail into the undeserved,
Troubles upon troubles upon glass upon globules.
This is the way I've always known I was encouraged
To fall in love, imperfections and all, the pearls of my spine
Exhausting to speak and to observe: he prevails despite
Negotiations I hope to double my chances for nothing.

May Mowing Clover

The art of mowing's paltry craft. I prolong
The misery of procrastination through weed
And thistle, kin to artichoke, edible if you peel
Away the spines. Two weeks and one rain suffice
To rear a bed of clover in the west back yard,
A matching patch southeast, but few dandelions
Out front: last spring's labors with a pronged tool
Paid off. By noon in May it's tricky to begin,
The heat's sinuous waves already floating
Above the street, but today I tied age-stained
Running shoes and donned shorts for the job
I still find novel, never having practiced it
Till renting a neat house in a neighborhood
Where the tune of one mower moves all residents
To shame till the whole street's a cacophony
Of buzzing blades and the air smells next to sex:
Those cut green juices flowing fresh. Priming
The mower was tough enough. I leaned close to hear
The trickle and could not: I may be deafened
In middle age, or lack right touch on rubber button,
Pressing too slow, or harsh, but finally, the gush,
And tug on cord sparked a bluish puff of oil smoke,
Staggering rumble, roar: we were off. I loved
To worry each blade to ground: is it wrong
To tear spent daffodils? Should they die back
Naturally to season next spring's blossoms?
What of wood chips ringing Bradford pear
For looks, now grown over in some species

That shears bleached at tips? Might they dull
The mower blades? Shaving the tight squeeze
Between carport posts and Toyota challenges aim
And patience, but to fail means weed-eating,
Plugging the long cord, which flops from outlet
At the slightest brush with impediment: best
To take one's chances early, and I did, with success
Due to parking closer to the wall than I dared
Last year or year before. Live and learn,
By accident: it works. I fancy the pattern
That tracks lawn's perimeter, shunting cut grass
Inwards to mow and mow again—technique
For those who own no mower bag and neither
Care to rake, as it reduces waste to finest mulch
(So I was told). Yet I've read that one must not
Repeat a pattern long for fear of forming ruts,
Or lumps; so at the center I reversed my path
And let the clippings blow across the ever-widening
Tidied spot: I would say "expanse," but it's not.
I felt bold. When blades met wood, I breasted crunch,
Squinted against splinters that flicked my shins.

The front was done in record time. I'd opened
The gate to obviate the need to prime
And start a second time, but wind had blown it
Shut: I pried it with the mower's nose
And set in under shrubs in need of pruning.
I razored crocuses, only their striped spikes

Left from early March. I darted twixt
The plastic plugs of sewage overflow valves
And managed both to leave them whole and carve
The grass to even length. But the worst: that thick
Blossoming clover, honey waiting to happen,
White heads bobbing host to ladybugs and those
Few bees I welcome, survivors of this era's
Industrial blights and parasites: how history
Changes us, since once I feared sting's poison
And now their loss if bees attack in vengefulness.
I paced ox-like behind the laboring motor,
Slow: speed chokes the mower's undercarriage,
Wet chew in clumps. The moist stalks, decapitated,
Lay down long, did not spring up. They'd ruin
The even look I worked for, my punishment
For letting them grow—but I would feed the bees
And shirk landlords' chastisements, if only
I had the nerve. I trimmed in, edging, up, down,
Across, back, and each time watched two honeybees
Grip meaty flowers till the last. They disappeared
A minute, but by my next pass, having circled—
Squared—the lawn, they'd returned and found more
Fodder, to which they clung with hunger, tenacity,
Furred legs quivering on stalk. Through the vines
Along the fence, past the concrete turtle beneath
Which a pencil-slim snake coiled to whip away,
Exposed, and the desiccated dog turds stashed
In shaded corner near last summer's morning

Glory trellis, I forged on, and still clover rose,
Shrunken in zone, but enough for bees, that pair
I imagined twin sisters, workers, not so busy as me:
It had to happen. Either I would leave
A swatch of bee-graze or I would not. I would
Breathe courage of unconvention, know neighbors'
Glares, or bow like slashed stems and wait to rise up.
You guess how I chose. By the time I reached
That foot-wide blaze of nectared bloom, I saw
Not two bees but four, easy to count clustered
Stubborn among remains. Cowardly, I nudged
The mower across their feeding ground, and finished,
Dispatching a ladybug or two, since they fly
Sluggish. Not the honeybees. They looped up
By my face. They did not land. Then vanished
And I released the mower handle and heard
The engine die. The smell of lawn enchanted me.
Already I'd mastered my hesitation: it danced
Like a wagging bee into the sky of human pride.

Weekends Only

That water-sprinkler's wagging the dog—
Black-saddled terrier trotting after old man in orange cap,
Also avoiding the glittering wave wetting a patchy lawn.
Bets are off whether it grows thicker—
Better, at least, than the man's head when he whisks off cap
And scratches. Dog follows suit, though it's early
For fleas, and next to step out for a draught of afternoon's
A youngish woman in striped sweater, hands at rest in pockets.
It's Saturday, which shows in every stance and gesture—
Nowhere to rush off, for once, and a sky that says
Stand still and feel who you are, now and tomorrow.
Everything's familiar, even the doves trampling porch-
Potted fern for a safer clutch than last year's,
Which blew down, remember?—tragic eggs, cracked under-
Foot, beside driveway. We always hope for fresh
Beginnings when the air's so light it hoists
Lawn sprinkler's mist like a wing, and dog, doves,
Men in caps, and daughters live through minutes
Tipped eggshell white, green as unfurled leaves.

Story Box

That year is the locked box. The smart box,
Sheer sides polished with rock salt.
Dreary dark box lit red in one corner,
Air thick with fixer, wet photos dripping dry,
Ghost box, soul box, somebody stole your soul
Box, snapped your photo when you looked
Lost. Map box, get on the road box,
Step on the gas box, all routes lead nowhere
Box, motel box, bedspread box,
Man who clasped you in his arms box,
He might've been a boxer, with round biceps
And shiny shorts, shark box, you wandered
The beach box, snorted coke from an ivory box,
Rolled a c-note, coughed into the box, where
Was the sneeze box, tissue box, tits and ass box,
They used to call pussy "box," *don't call it that* box,
Don't touch it box, *don't get anywhere near me* box:
This, the old news sealed in the carved box.

I was seventeen. If the world were a box
And the directions to sail seas simple,
Handwritten on rectangular paper, a document
Of import just for me, you could wrest it
From my hands and pry inside, and good luck
Facing me, in my halter top worn not in beauty
But grim duty, that year I tried to go blank
Like a slat in a pine box, stash box,
The Reader's Digest condensed book
I hollowed with a razor to hide my secret

Possessions: it stayed empty. That year
I meant to swap my child's love for horses
For a woman's passion for men. Once I lay
On the ground, naked, gazing across the angles
Of my body, concave belly between hipbones
And below, grimacing, a man's face. Beside me,
In a station wagon mottled with junk yard mold,
My friend Robin, a mature fourteen, *getting fucked*.
I stared up with the man's face buried,
No pleasure in the sharpness of his tongue's touch,
And no one saw me though I saw all in shame.
Robin's breasts bloomed bigger, her face prettier.
The more handsome man, notable for ponytail
And hairy wrists, fucked her. All the players
Know their place in the race and to come in last,
Never to come at all, is why I ran fast, pleading
To strip and endure the stippling mouth
And pretend. I kept old letters in a box,
Men had written of my body, who were they
Writing to? My mother read their tuneless
Chants, I knew when she called me
A prostitute. So had she been, she recalled
The signs, we prospered poorly. Who's safe
Indoors when the doors are hung on hinges?
Who despises her past when it's locked
In its warped-lid asbestos box? The back
Of my hand slapped like a square paddle.
The fingers jutted like wires. The mirror

Inside sold my face back to me, desperate
To give and receive. Car up on blocks.
Listen to the talk, soft gossip that mocks.
I knew how to sit a horse, speak the commands
Walk and *trot*, and I could ride a course of jumps,
The horse's iron toes knocking poles
In parabola so they rocked in the rusted cups.
My mother had sold her body to buy them
So I followed like a colt—that's the story
I made up. Take the papers from the box.
Stay awake to read them. Try not to feel
Too shocked or bored at the female drama.

There's a silver latch on the box top. Breathe
On it, dampen it, wipe away your fingerprints
So I don't know who's trailed me like a colt,
A goat, spun like a top, a gyroscope,
Or sharpened a speculum to see up my twat.
Don't be shocked, take back the reflection,
Just forget, I didn't say it, if I did I didn't mean it.
I was pure pretense, rolling on grassy earth,
Spread apart like a girl with a job to do.
I didn't have the looks but Robin did
And I had to prove I had something.
I don't know what happened to her.
There are only so many stories in this box.
If you fish it's a tackle box. If you cook
The fish, an icebox. If you store forks

And spoons you line it with felt.
If you dance at a ball you line it with finer felt,
And the diamonds shine, silver glistens
Untarnished. If you leave the country,
Believing you are dying, you burn the box.
You open the stove to stow it in flame
And the story of a hand slapping your good-looking
Ass on the way to the shadowy spot gets lost.
If you go to war you need an ammunition box.
If you start a business you need a file box.
If you work as a plumber you need a toolbox.
If you want to pretend none of this happened
You break the box, memorize its contents, pour
Gasoline, strike a match and stand back, rush back,
To the year you were seventeen, or I was,
And change came upon you like demons freed
From Pandora's box so for years
You trapped them, in nets and boxes, wings
Like the wings of bats, eyes like the eyes
Of fathers and mothers, hands like the hands
Of men who have no hands, mouths nipping
Between your legs like fish you can't catch,
Flying fish, fish swimming upstream,
Prostitutes men describe as stinking up
Their cars with the reek of cock and twat.
They want clean boxes, edges set straight, craft
For their pleasure, buying and throwing back,
Fish everybody says they'd never eat:

That girl is lost. Her body is lying like paper
In the grass, a box beside her, she's reaching for it,
She should've burned it. She never wanted you
To know, but as with all forms of knowledge
And all beginnings, stopping strictly
Demands never starting, never the first idea.

Travel Plans for Social Outcasts

There's no good in this, I thought each mile
Like onionskin the Toyota's tires unpeeled—
But I wanted home. Asheville's naked bikers
Leering out motel room doors froze forever
In the rear view mirror and time sped
Like a scooter. I imagined Sara coursing back
The opposite direction, due east to my 40 West,
Sun drenching us both after our innocent
Rendezvous, married homeschooler and
Escaped academic believed to be *too mean*
For men, odds are, closeted lesbian—this insight
Thanks to undergrads who don't know not to
Talk. It's sad at the center of an empty
Universe, i.e. university gossip, small town,
Rightwing state in need of unholy martyrs.
I burn like any saint or better.
God knows what the desk clerk thought,
In Asheville, aristocratic Indian beauty
With perfect British articulation, and though
I intended to complain about the biker
Strutting the parking lot in ass-crack shorts,
A man at the counter seemed likely
His friend so I abstained. Sara and I
Shared a cheap room and watched serial killer
Shows on the Learning Channel
Until I fell asleep on top of the remote
And she switched off the set so its red eye
Glowed a warning next morning when I woke,

Anxious about the weather, and flipped
Through newscasts till Paula Zahn's clenched
Tooth professionalism informed of the latest
Videotape: a woman guilty of child abuse,
Slapping her daughter at a shopping mall.
I might as well have been a cop myself
When Sara said the bitch deserved
Everything she got and I stopped
That talk fast with feminist analysis.
What a way to treat my oldest friend.
I'm too mean for men, but Sara took it
Well, briefly wide-eyed, later thankful
I teach new perspectives. She said so,
Verbatim. I could get it on videotape.
Anyway, it was great to breakfast on waffles
And scrambled eggs with my friend
Who enjoys my corrections. We smoked
Cigarettes and compared notes on losing
Weight and progress towards menopause,
Hers unguessable due to birth control shots.
Not me, I rely on plain meanness to prevent
Sperm entering the system or even my front door.
Whatever works: that's how I see it. We said
Goodbye at a convenience store where
She bought Bit O' Honey and I chose Diet Coke,
Caffeine for the road, and tested the air
In my tiny tires because the rims jut, not like
A biker's belly overhanging shorts

But that's what comes to mind once you've faced
That vista, swallowing metaphor like vaginas
Of misogynistic myth. What swallowed time
As I drove west? Rolling Stones cd—remind me
To get rid of that—or joint I smoked or need
To sleep in my own bed or fear of strangers,
Like the toothless white-shocked interloper
Who approached me smirking *God Bless*
At the gas pumps, West Memphis—Arkansas
Side—with a predictable lie about an alternator,
A family stranded, and twenty-six more dollars
Needed. I handed over a ten to buy my peace,
But the other women he pitched smiled big
And begged off: *My husband holds the money.*
At least I scowled. And did not lie. Which
Enchanted my thoughts five hundred miles
Driving me past West Memphis before sunset,
Mountains behind like a dream in the sky
I'd drifted down from, winding right, left,
South, west, sinuous ribbons of interstate,
Eighteen-wheelers lumbering loud giants
Decked out in lights like a gay bar
But don't tell the drivers, who think
When a boy gives them a blowjob
They're all just desperate. They're right,
Too. Anyway, I thought if I ached
Too much I'd pull off for the night,
But when my gas pedal foot throbbed

I rubbed the tendon on the bony top
And when my sides cramped I leaned
As if still sticking the curves of the Great
Smokies and when my head pulsed
I rustled a roach from the ashtray
And hunkered behind the steering wheel
So no truckers would get ideas. You can't
Trust them. They're all conservative.
I shoved the poetry cd in the dash machine
And clicked until cut 17, Robert Lowell
Intoning "Skunk Hour," and his choked voice
Had me in tears by the second stanza,
Undoubtedly why he's loathed by scholars
Everywhere I've been, which isn't far.
The academic equivalent of a West Memphis
Gas station and miles of irrigated soybean
Fields, landing strips, and billboards,
Girls' photos captioned DO YOU KNOW
WHO MURDERED ME? And me sailing
Through the ribs of the plains, burning
Like a Comanche arrow, my face wet
With Lowell's stoic jokes and the loss
Of my ten dollars and pride at my refusal
To lie, worth at least that much: to be female,
Unmarried, and forty-six is to give up
Money to lying men. *Lie back and enjoy it*,
They used to say, I was never sure who,
Having felt it when it seemed I might say no

To anything. The other women at the gas pumps
Said no but lied. I said yes but did not.
They smiled, I scowled: I work this equation
To the story of our defeated lives, intricate
Hairdos, thighs we try to *work off*
And have since youth, we fail and will
Till death melts them: *there's no good*
In this, I thought, and was right, but I sped
Anyway, and where did the day go?
I imagined with a start that I was dead,
Killed shortly after emerging from Asheville
In a collision I'd never remember,
Now returning home in dream,
Bearing down too fast for mortal fact.
Here, already, was the Muskogee Turnpike.
How would I prove myself dead or alive?
If I glanced into my lap and saw bare bone?
If I tossed five quarters in the toll basket
And heard no clink of change on wire
But the light smiled green-ball anyway?
Lying like married women who want to keep
The cash? Paula Zahn's cruel eyes flashing
DEATH TO ALL WOMEN BUT ME?
No, there are no reliable tests for life.
What's known can be dreamed
In the afterlife, if that's how it works,
And who knows until they're there?
Who knows they're back in Oklahoma
When the wind blows everywhere?

With those options, one only knows to go,
So I drove, headlights exploding
In the rearview like punk fireworks,
They'll blow your head off, my body's
Murmured pains mapped all over thought
On the grand scale, invisible inside
My short-clipped head—students all say
I'm a lesbian—and thirteen hours down,
Fourteen, I tracked it in one day,
Like a reincarnated trucker who cannot die
Again because I wanted home so badly
I didn't care how I needed to be away,
The storefront churches harboring
Damn fool cowboys who'll ride a bull
Till he breaks their skulls with cloven hooves,
Sunflowers blooming wild in August,
The Osage orange hurling its threat
To spiders, knuckled green grenades
You stash behind your toilet to freshen
Your house of webs, or so it's sold, the sky
To whose first star I wish each evening, always
The same hope, same embarrassing secret,
The sky, rusty earth, ragweed, groundnut,
Cedar, whatever makes my eyes itch,
The reek of skunks, even the armadillos,
The sorry spectacle of my life cloistered
In the talk of the lonely and smug who need
Someone, something, to hold themselves
Above—like mountains. Like Gatlinburg,

Dollywood, tourist traps, talk's cheaper
Than a room there, so you might as well
Stay in Oklahoma and fix your eyes
On the moving target, what's her problem?
Why is she so mean? She wants to be home.
I wanted it, and was close, and I was careful
On 51 not to speed through Yale where so many
Have been ticketed and harassed,
And not one light shimmered inside
The Housing Authority complex,
Not one light blinked on at any farm
Or in any doublewide, not one car crawled
The two-lane besides mine, and home,
Hateful when I'm there, terrifying me
The seven years it took to turn me into it,
Each cell of my bones and skin, each doomed
Handful of organ meat in my belly,
Turned over like the odometer on an old car,
A junker, home was the junker, home was me,
Home was what I hated but could not leave
For long. Then I pulled into College Gardens,
My neighborhood, with its brisk toy houses
And sleeping dolls, breath caught
In its throat on the cusp of summer and fall,
And I parked my car in the driveway,
I unfolded my legs from the cramped compartment,
I must've been a living body, I walked
To my front door and twisted the key in the lock,
And the sound could not have been anything but
True, the pressure of the stiff lock the force

Of material reality, and the friend waiting there,
Who had made me soup, simmered it all night
Waiting for me, was not a phantom,
Not any of the names I've heard her called,
And for a while I could be glad about my place,
Feeding my hunger, resting my living marrow
Inside my living bone, until the boredom
And the grief started over again next morning,
And I had to write a poem to kill it, or keep it
Alive, or both, like now. This is the surge
Of my perennial death and reliable resurrection,
And you who listen are a trucker who bears down
In my mirror blinding me, or an abuser
Of children, a venomous newscaster, an old friend,
Or someone believed to be unlike anyone else:
You catch my drift. I don't trust anybody.
I make sure to tell the truth against the common
Background of anguished mimesis, everyone
Unselfconscious in drag, learned books
Directing us towards it as surely as bad tv
In motel rooms where bikers refuse to shut
Their doors and women anachronistically
Coiffed, bulging, bludgeoning blonde
Bouffant, pace the sidewalks wondering,
Who is this stranger, how does she bear up
Under our longing looks and our loathing?
And, whoever she is, maybe just me, suffers
The close embrace of the automobile's
Tight cell racing the nation's rough arteries
Where so many before her have died.

Tourmaline

Last night, rummaging through her jewel box, velvet
Lining thinning like once-lush coiffured jeweler's
Hair, I counted out brooches, bracelets, necklace—
Just one. Leaving the rest for farther, longer
Evenings, when, as the twilight guarded darker
I could figure in dream however long joy's
Fantasies fanned out peacock tails, I finished
Circling my throat in tourmaline: glass rainbow,
Watermelon pink, greenest rind where fourteen
Karats bracketed gemstone's crusty pillow
And spilled upwards like snake spine, wriggling chain, thin,
Measured nonetheless. *Mother wore this*—simple
Honorific I whispered as if hearing
Her voice, not my own. Not much difference, lately:
Her life, mine, nothing sacred symbolizing
Either daughterly habits—bookish tempers—
Or maternal inflections, décor, Southern
Accents. What can I say? I feigned her gesture
As I fastened the necklace, fingers slipping
The latch, collarbone stable ledge for clipping
What she never let me touch when she could've
Watched me imitate, dress my face in kindred
Framing: absolute? Not yet. This necklace, name
Of the qualifying attire, late costume.
Once I learned not to divulge such marked details.
Then she left me with gemstones, fabric boxes,
Duties, revelry hers alone till absent
Time passed. Now, see, it's mine and will be, it seems,

For good. Daughterless, I'm the end of preening
Before looking-glass, wearing tourmaline down.

Cloudtime

Slow autumn Saturdays leave little time
For methods greater than the grayest sky
To hover over stricken souls, or crimes,

Or other scenes of loss, confusion, high
Despair, like nothing else all year: it seems
An afternoon's to live so long to die

In shoals of cloud, not drowned so much as dreamed.
For instance, I'm unmoving from my chair
All day, despite the promise of thin beams

Too frail to name *sunshine* and also rare
Through opened blinds I've watched for hours and closed
Only to pry apart when next my lair

Is lit in streaks like pencil leads or those
Glittering shards sent down by shooting stars.
I check the firmament for hope, suppose

Nothing is much improved, spot a new car
Parked near the neighbor's door and, soured, return
To proper waste of time so meanly marred

By tedious weather as to rate what's spurned
Even by she who mostly takes what comes.
That would be me. I mean I've seldom burned

What I could somehow keep. I count the numb
Minutes, which tick like rain on windowpanes—
But there's no flowing in the silent drum

Of gray October—dry, and deep, the grains
Of harvest waiting, gourds, fat apples, grapes
Withered to woody vines some gardener trained

To grip a trellis until corkscrew-shaped.
So much to think about I must not stir.
Instead I count, I yawn, I notice drape

Of fabric and of cloud, and time's soft whirr
Like insects winding down to winter, death
Or hibernation, hives' long sleep assured

Of waking at the first intake of breath
In spring: so I imagine now, to pass
The afternoon, or hold so still it lets

Me pass, stark shadow on the dying grass
When I stand up to stretch and stare outdoors,
At last, full profile through the misted glass

Of my back window, when nothing more
Alive than light bulbs casts my silhouette
Where all day I've refused to walk, so bored

With weekend's disappointments I could dread
Anything better—senseless, I know.
For this I might as well have stayed in bed

And let my dreams provide the all-day show.
Too bad, to pine so hard for light and joy
A whole day's gone to bitter guilt, with no

Respite in work or rest, a grown-up toy
Like a new tv, maybe: maybe not.
Was this Saturday's gray my shabby ploy

For empty griping? *Maybe: maybe not*—
And even that evasive answer leaves
Stasis gray-streaked above my head, to nod

With grief, or punishment, its weighty sheaves.

Counting Change

The watermelon's velvet red split oval geode
Propped upended against the uncut, garnet vinestones.

Tractor trawling brickish dust balloon cloud, hauling
Late August, long wait, midseason, nothing now—

I mean nothing. You caught me squatting
Over my own blood, torrent, thumblong, thumbthick

Clots so I groaned, knowing, foreseeing coagulated
Velvet, physician's forehead gleaming above mask, harvest,

Internet photography, halved organs, captioned *lush hyperplastic
Fronds*, and my desire reduced to survivalist

Lust: patient child I was, determined, promising
I'll take what I want, without warning

The passage of time, deadlines extended only
Enough for next comers, newcomers, full sails

On Topsail Island, drive home sunburnt, arriving
Before dark: I remember but cannot restore.

Body, stay by me, enclose my soul
Another long time, I beg, hanging back.

It's summer, nobody's accomplished much, forgive us
For wasting the abundant gifts, fruits, commercialism,

Heart, squashtop, richripe, raging discrepancy in story
Repeated to police investigators incantatory *lalala tra*

Fooled me fooled you I want latitude
Longitude devil cake everything I gave up.

O my solitary terrors. I laugh them,
From over my shoulder small, tidy, distant

As your death, scheduled during my absence
To spare us both. Bring a spoon.

The filling's delicious. Vanilla bean pudding crusted
In banana chocolate, lips brushing pursestrings, obeisance,

I was so scared I couldn't speak.
I who had always blurted black seeds

Like watermelon's truth couldn't interrupt the panting
Rhythm, my termination undeniably due, no longer

What somebody else wanted against my unstoppable
Concrete will, veined marble categories of triumph,

Likely stories, apologies. I knelt. I gushed.
I ate. All night and all year

The suffering of bottles in the window,
My earliest memory, soon to count last.

The Apparent Suicide of My Former Husband

His third wife called to say he'd been found dead.

We'd emailed after he forced her to swallow eighty Depakote
and smashed her in the head with a wine bottle.
She was gathering evidence about his past violence.
She said it would make it easier to file for a restraining order.

Now she told me of his body found in the hall of the loft
he'd moved to; no signs of harm to the corpse
or forced entry at door or window; no heart attack.

The last time he and I talked he shouted *I'm a cipher to you.*
Maybe no one will crack his case now either,

beyond autopsy: his ribs pried open, diagnosis—
cirrhosis, not enough to kill.

                          The trouble with wives is
we want a reliable man. If we've slept around too much
already
it's a relief to be off the market.
                         It's not supposed to turn
into an abattoir, pig's guts twining at our ankles
wall to wall in the apartment he's been banished to,
                         fist and spittle flying.

I dreamed his body flayed on a hook two nights

after he died. I woke angry he'd crept in, twirling
the martial arts swords he collected, the thirteen unlucky
guitars, and a tune carried like a tun, splashing
his big boots.
          I was young for him once, and made him fix
things like a proper man, broken legs, dinner, tumbling souls.

          So when I imagined the suicide scene
I brought to bear every loft I've seen, Halloween
decorations, angel fur ghastly in doorways, costumes
clasping the torsos of men I'd never desire.

I imagined his empty shell so thick I would've breathed it ripe with life.
          What if he shrieked *You should've left me dead?*

Young lover scalding a decade of woe, goat with pipes,
unpaid electric bill butterflied down a drain, Madonna
centerfold crushed behind the sofa: how can you love
a man like that, dead?

I'm sorry I couldn't twist him right, tease him off his feet
to spin. He thought he was fine as he was
          until the split second air vamoosed
and it was no joke,
not a squeal of fingers on strings or time for goodbye.

Now I'm on my knees blowing in the pelt of his shoulders.
I'm shearing a lock for my necklace.

I'm going to seal it under glass
to be reminded of his birthday in the month of virgins.

I never imagined us old together,
even when I thought it was all my fault,
not the accurate premonition of more than another wife,
more than a long time far away, more than I would've dared
to guess,
                and much more blood than I wanted,

no matter what I might've furiously declared.

Elegy Enumerating the Sins of Shopping

Now that he's on my mind again after ten years of forgetting,
I have this unwelcome picture in my head:
I'm sitting him down and telling him why I shopped so much
I earned, one year, a V.I.P. credit card at my favorite store,
A chain called Palais Royal. In my fantasy we perch in chairs
Like those where he waited near the perfumed entrance
Of Palais Royal while I browsed and tried on and paid for
My purchases. The chairs were shaped like cups, beveled
On top like a china lip, upholstered in striped sheen,
A nub to the weave like raw silk—probably imitation,
To hold up under the haunches of husbands
Accompanying women in their prime years who sought
To become real women, women a man could fantasize of—
Which is necessary for real women, to be dreams.
In my fantasy I tell the truth and he listens
As he never did those buried years of credit card debt,
One-sided arguments and graduate school, and his mother
Loathing me for my ambitions, visiting us in our rental house
And turning her face away. She loved her son so much
She could speak of nothing else, except money.
In my fantasy I tell what I only filtered through experience
This belated afternoon, weeks after his mysterious death,
Years after our lives joined in a pretense of passion
I tried to titillate with clothing: the excessive trends of the '80's,
Geometric prints, big shoulder pads, boas and earrings,
Polka-dots Madonna might've worn in a video. I knew
He liked Madonna because I'd found the Playboy centerfold
Stashed under the sofa in the living room where the dogs slept.

We argued, and he lied, claiming it wasn't his: maybe
The landlord entered when we were out of town and left it,
Masturbating and tossing it aside. After I divorced him
He confided to friends that I was paranoid schizophrenic,
His evidence that I believed strangers trespassed to self-abuse.
None of that matters now, except as curiosity, since he is,
Incredibly, dead, and I'm stalling on returning his third wife's
Third phone call, though she probably has more information,
Insight into what he swallowed, if anything, that killed him.
The more I know the deader he gets. Already he's so dead
I can think of little else but the mystery story
Of his body found and nobody having a clue. No violence,
No broken locks. Only his hunched corpse, hunkering
Broad back I remember slouching in the striped chairs
Of Palais Royal while I played at signaling I adored him,
Decking my young body in lace I wanted him to finger
On my thighs, snazzy prints and pink-dyed chick-
Feathers and whatever else I could charge on my V.I.P. card.
All for his sake, couldn't he tell? Didn't he desire a real woman,
Wrapping herself for him to open, a gift of me from me
Signed *me for you, love, and I am costly*? He did not.
Appraising myself in the mirror and finding a decent imitation
Of a desirable woman as featured in fashion pix, even
Centerfolds, yet failing to work the magic in his eyes,
So that now I would take the punishment twice, his failure
To love and his rage at the debt, bills daily in mailbox—
Disappointed, I lost the dream of myself
In tenderness and patience. The dream I conjured then

Returns unbidden now, sitting him down in the teacup chair:
Darling, I have something to tell you, and what I tell you must forgive.
But I gave it up like a shopping bag wadded in the trash
To hide price tags, as if that could work, and it never did:
Price tags lingered longer than my tender love.
Yet I live on. And he does not, though born years later than I,
Once reason to twist my hips into fabrics guaranteed
To arouse while the hips were slim. It seemed worth
Every desperate penny, student loan checks I repay today:
He does not live to assist me and if he did would not.
If there's money to be had from his passing it will not pass to me.
I will not travel to his grave to weep or to desecrate.
In my fantasy he lives and I make him understand—but the fear is
I'll keep learning. I will puff up like a dry cleaner's bag
Draped over a sequined gown, and there will be no end
To knowing. His body will molder, still denying me, my folly,
Femininity, rayon, cotton, dotted swiss, bust darts, garter belts,
Stockings seamed in rhinestones—I bought for him
And he didn't know. He somehow thought me selfish.

Stereotype

Greater use of the Internet was associated with declines in participants'
communication with family members in the household, declines in the size
of their social circle, and increases in their depression and loneliness…
      --American Psychologist
      http://www.apa.org/journals/amp/amp5391017.html

That aspect of the male body requiring jeans
To hang low on the hips, sagging in the ass, bagging
At the knees, a belt securing the waist below the waist,
Below the overhang—I won't name it.
Even this bright first day of December, the man
Strolling home down West Arrowhead, glancing
Where I crouch on the edge of the Adirondack chair
On my porch—then, when I look up, glancing
Away—it's hard to feel anything but contentment.
He appears to be "working class," judging from his attire,
And married. In this neighborhood, you can bank on
A guess separating college students from their elders,
Though in this state the transition from lone caste
To coupled happens early for most: it's old-fashioned,
Sweet as an auctioneer's patter on a Sunday afternoon,
Hateful with secrets like the Cherokee woman murdered
The week after 9/11 by boys who mistook her skin.
I run slighter risks but don't go out except for work
And grocery shopping. A bird feeder dangles from a cord
Above my head. Earlier, sparrows tangled for millet,
All show, spread wings, tenacity of the extra-
Small, dull plumage and zero self-awareness, pecking
Order no subject for discussion in their survivalist culture.
Indoors, though, my computer tells another story,

Incredible from this perspective, saffron sun, tarnished
Asphalt driveway, trash bags poised for morning
Pick-up, the memory of stars: an online argument
That lasted weeks, in words loose as flour in a sack,
And what I wrote to finish: *You win.* I had asserted
That a woman spotted shopping was likely married
To a rich man, judging from her clothes and body,
The neighborhood, too, "Quail Springs": you know the type.
Or *stereotype*, what someone claimed I'd spoken, and it did
Not go over. Stereotyped, as with double speakers,
I who had guessed and she who insisted I should not.
Together, we stereotyped, from Seattle, from Stillwater,
And across the nation screens glowed midnight blue
Through the retinas of readers who might otherwise
Have crept like hungry cats into shrubbery to catch
The murmur of sleeping birds. If I was wrong to guess
A woman's life from a glimpse, should I or anyone offer
Herself in secret public places, the Internet, to strangers:
What are we missing? The moment when summer's stalk
Dries and the whisper of grass stems shakes out
One drop and rattles? Or shattered robins' eggs ground
Under raccoon's heel, or opossum's, or tomcat's, belled
Or not: the one on my street is. I'm asking if it's possible
To know the life of the sidewalk crack when all you do is talk,
Type, *stereotype*, twinned typists, coast to heartland,
The illusion of rising on steam of language,
When nobody's going anywhere in fact. Except
A man strolling home from work. What did he think

When he glanced my way, huddled in December sun?
Something, I hope, even if, arriving at his own door,
He called to his wife that he noticed someone wrong,
Breathing demon nicotine, hair too short, likely lesbian,
And the lawn not mowed in proper time so it's stuck
Unkempt for the season: he'd be right, mostly. I allow
He's human, thus curious, lacking in perfect insight,
Subject to judgment. I pity his patient wife, impatient
Daughter, whoever's there: I'll never know. But I'll know more
From watching him and other neighbors and their dogs,
Bicycles, flowerpots, and Christmas trees twinkling
In windows, than from that human habit, mouse-clicking
"Enter," so the infinite scroll of Babel floats where we want it.
Better to guess the marital status of any stranger walking,
Glancing, heading home, the old way, on foot, forsaking
The shadow as long as it takes to turn the corner,
See the shabby house still square on its lot, and hurry on.

Regretful of Error

The merest rise in the sidewalk might friction a sneaker toe
To hang behind the body's momentum.
This small flaw in motion's assembly, akin to the stick
Of gears, embarrasses the flow of strolling, joints
And levers merging in rhythm to make the pace.
I occupy such a bag of bones, am nimble
Bearing grocery sacks or balancing wheelbarrow
Handles, backyard beast of burden until I stumble,
Singing to myself as the neighbors slam
Windows or listen for sour notes, victory to random
Rage, which exists despite sense or apology.
In public I rely on intuition to stay me upright
As a sail in narrow wind. I'm held like a fork
Between fingers. I prod like a stage prop
To crowd's front, hoping they know where they're going.
I'm visible as a sofa the cat sharpened claws on.
I'm the woman who pretended to control fate
When deafness drowned out the voices of everyone
But fear. Do I look all right? Can you tell what I did
Last night? Salt of the sea, fuchsia fuzz of champagne
Mimosa, syllables I hummed as if I possessed
The hoax of incantation? I measure my features
Against excuses and famous sayings, advertisements
For perfection and the fly in the sunburn salve.
It's one pratfall after another, tumbler in a torn leotard,
The story I tell about the stories I told before
Telling the last one to the last laugh of the last listener,
Who spotted me in a throng, paused, and rushed on

Till an ankle turned in a divot like a cue ball leaping
From felt. In my dream we fell and rose again
Clothed in beauty. I reminded myself to count hopes
As facts so when everything went wrong I'd see
Smiles gracious as a vase of burnt roses, ash
Rubbed into cheeks and lips and veins of marble.

Regretful of Error 2

Stamp collecting demands tweezers and a lens,
Ring binders, plastic envelopes, a corneal transplant, and taste
For etchings of queens' faces, and tigers',
Pandas, sailboats, flags rippling in poisoned wind.

Times have changed. A friend who outswam me from channel
To channel begs to be seated for the sake of her trick knee.
The city of Dubuque recruits young women with baccalaureate
Degrees to occupy stone towers above the river,

From which they declare they profit teaching anatomy
Of centipedes to former prisoners of war who mature
To believe no one's efforts to comprehend the universe
Equal the iconic. The rings of Saturn circle their necks and elbows.

Middle-aged men experience gout at higher rates than their piscine
Counterparts. Acorns crunch beneath cane tips on the avenue.
We dreamed of fame for jockeys besides us, yet here we are on the front
Page licking ice cream cones—strawberry swirl, thanks!

Would you take it back for a loan? Your automobile's vast tires
Dashed a signature. You crawled between the thighs of library statuary,
The shape of its calves amusing you, pleasingly altered,
As if you had consorted with the enemy or consumed the blood

Of goats with their permission. The pain, the pain. Oh, ceaselessly secreted
Away for lack of interest and now perceptible as a carbon scar.
A young man in a black t-shirt imprinted Small Town
Gay Bar seats himself at a table piled with Lego palm trees

And seconds your self-pity. After you regale him with information
He'd prefer to ignore, royal pupae burst forth moths.
It happens. There's more later. And no turning back
On what turns out to be everything but a glass avenue. The stamps

For mailing packages are as flat as a fistula. They sally forth,
Depicting journey. Children are awfully grown-up these days,
But they still talk too much about what they're planning to become—
Butlers or rubber masks or pontoon boats or a bellyache.

Ouch, it hurts. One minute they're toppling from the hands
Of their ancestors and the next they're real as coral snakes.
Old age, I mean. Your companions' faces seemingly radiant
In nests of white fluff, not high-grade styrofoam but biological waste.

You remove the cap from the well and peer down the crooked shaft.
It's moving, whatever it is. Its legs and belly gleam in a strand of dusk.
If you don't stop screaming you'll never make it out alive,
To spend the rest of eternity deformed on the corners

Of envelopes whirling through machines and arriving right on time.
But on the other hand the longer your voice challenges perfume
And reason, the more certain powerful forces will take a shine
To your last throes. That's what they mean when they shake your mitt

And congratulate you on how you were worth every minute.
Not like a giant but what you couldn't help—"being yourself,"
Someone optimistically offered, and someone else complained
That such comments wasted a perfectly adequate existence.

The Perspective of Distance

How do I walk? Heel to toe? Is the world arranged at right angles?

The long flat building where workers gather each morning.

The stable where girls lead dappled thoroughbreds with halters and ropes.

Even the road paved in black macadam dissolves to oak leaves.

You say this is the ordinary asserting itself. You won't look me in the eye.

You pull yellow gloves to your wrists and tilt the brim of a cap on your forehead.

It's the way you take revenge for my neglecting to prepare you for the sky,

the difference in the light over the hillsides. Yes, it's blue, and it stays

blue no matter the weather, which is, I promise, the name of sameness.

Other things change. If you're running a business, a soda shop for instance,

and a letter drops from the sign, you may not climb the ladder to nail it back.

The children playing marbles may not change the rules they were taught.

It might turn out that no one remembers who laid the circle of string.

But it would take a direct hit to the sun to pull a shade over the open sky.

You could walk away from me, defying the last word and the first word,

I could watch the prints your heels cut in the dust, and the sky would gape,

not like an astonished eye, not like a bird's beak, more like an unstitched wound.

Coupled

The neck's crest bridges to the pricked ears.
The ears flick back when the neck rises.
I've read the loose-ring snaffle doubles
The hands' gestures to the horse's tongue:
Gloves mute their randomness, uncontrolled
Twitches of the fingers, blood's pulse.
I bought lilac nylon, suede-palmed to stick
To reins' leather slick with mare's sweat.
It lathers between her thighs on hot days,
Like today, as the video shows at home
In air-conditioning while I watch myself,
And her, working to learn. My technique's
Flaws bewilder us both: the ears flick back
When the neck rises. The back hollows,
The hocks drive out behind, the lumbosacral
Joint drops forward flexion, and the touch
Of my legs to her barrel offends, as the ears
Tell, and the neck, which, when correct,
Arches along the crest's length, the thick mane
Loose to the left, lifting in stride, bent
Like the tall grass through which a bull snake
Roiled, once, at the mare's feet, escaping
The wellhouse shade where last spring it shed
Skin. Neither of us flinched. We're bold
From weeks of training's concentration,
So I think back years, to lessons, horse shows,
Abandoned hopes, my belief I lacked
The talent, and know, now, decades late,

It was all wrong, including evaluation
Of error, and my life on top of bad riding
And worse guessing: I can't say I should've
Known but could've, since now, middle-aged,
Daily saddling the mare bought cheap
To relive old passions, ambitions, in secret
Dreams, I have gone on—gone and done it.
Sometimes, right. Her stiff side: right,
Meaning she is loath to stretch her left
But will, urged, considered, across the mowed
Bermuda pasture, mosquitoes choiring to feed,
Wood bees' stumbling feints, red dust, red mud,
Shoulder-in, leg yield, half-pass, rudiments
Of flying change, and my nights reading
And staring myself to sleep with remote control,
Slow mo, stop action, checking suspension
At the trot, why does she flirt her jaw, why fling
White lather, is the neck soft, or stiff, and which
Is wrong? Which goes round? Do I dare claim
We've done it right? Now that winning doesn't
Matter except alone, solitary ethic of pace,
Straddle, and afternoon light? I claim it
By the moment, where it lives. One night I read,
I must feel where each leg steps, not looking,
And next day did. Cantering, slow, hooves
Clocking spokes of a wheel. One night I read,
When you think you should take, give. Next
Day did: poured from suede palm, shoulder,

Sunburned, curled fingers, elbow's rusty hinge,
And the neck, chestnut, wet with honest rain,
Bowed to the bit, seeking touch through slight
Tension, chewing down air to meet metal
I could hold before her, floating: I won't betray
My joy when, between my calves, sides swelled,
And beneath my seat, back bounded like a doe,
Or ocean's wave, or love, of self, of rightness,
Balance, motion, *everything*. I'd say the world
Should've been there when I promised her that
Inch of space I'd plundered years and in obliging
Heart she returned the favor and gifted
Like a spring from earth's center: I'd say it
But the world was there, stretching snakeskin,
Bridging mare's footfalls everywhere, me
Mounted midst black-eyed susans, Indian
Paintbrush, one horsepower, dirt road west
Where pickups blurred, speeding, oblivious, wrong
As I'd been minutes before, and overhead both
Hawk and great blue heron, united in sky,
Gazing down, away, sailing like the sun
On high, and in my hands the clink of snaffle
Speaking back, *soft, now, tongue, metal, forge*
The rest of our lives worthwhile, soft, now, coupled.

Acknowledgments

Grateful acknowledgment is made to the editors of the journals in which the following poems first appeared, sometimes in slightly different form:

Confrontation: The Well-Intentioned
Cortland Review: Topography
Crab Orchard Review: Envy This; Travel Plans for Social Outcasts
Cut Throat: A Journal of the Arts: The Apparent Suicide of My Former Husband
Eclectica: Oklahoma; Stereotype
Florida Review: Burned House with Swimming Pool; Counting Change
Hunger Mountain: We Couldn't Be True
Laurel Review: Come-Back Spell
Many Mountains Moving: Coupled
Oklahoma Today: Weekends Only
Parthenon West Review: Regretful of Error 2
POOL: Regretful of Error
Salamander: Autumn Uncovers the Tall of the Trees
Seattle Review: I Don't Want You to Take Off My Clothes; The Woman Who Sued Me
Smartish Pace: American Dream; My Horses and I; Swanky
Sweeping Beauty: Contemporary Women Poets Do Housework (University of Iowa Press): May Mowing Clover
The Journal: Dear Late Snowy Morning; Story Box
Tuesday: An Art Project: The Perspective of Distance
32 Poems: Tourmaline
Under the Rock Umbrella: Contemporary American Poets 1951-1977 (Mercer University Press): Cloudtime

"Coupled" was reprinted in *Cadence of Hooves: A Celebration of Horses*

"American Dream," "My Horses and I," "Oklahoma," "Dear Late Snowy Morning," "We Couldn't Be True," "Story Box," "Travel Plans for Social Outcasts," and "Coupled" were also published by Poetry West as a chapbook titled *Story Box*.

About the Author

Lisa Lewis's books include *The Unbeliever* (University of Wisconsin Press, Brittingham Prize), *Silent Treatment* (Penguin, National Poetry Series), and *Vivisect*, (New Issues Press). A chapbook titled *Story Box* was also published as winner of the Poetry West Chapbook Contest. Her work has appeared in numerous literary magazines, including *Kenyon Review*, *Washington Square*, *Third Coast*, *American Literary Review*, *Fence*, *Seattle Review*, and *Rattle*, as well as a Pushcart Prize anthology and two editions of *Best American Poetry*. She has also won awards from the *American Poetry Review* and the *Missouri Review*. She directs the creative writing program at Oklahoma State University and serves as poetry editor for the *Cimarron Review*.

www.ingramcontent.com/pod-product-compliance
Lightning Source LLC
Chambersburg PA
CBHW022029090426
42739CB00006BA/350